Hopping on the Number Line

Nancy Kelly Allen

ROURKE PUBLISHING

www.rourkepublishing.com

www.rourkepublishing.com

PHOTO CREDITS: Cover: © Jon Helgason, Ron Rutgers; Title Page: © Vichaya Kiatying-angsulee; Page 3, 21: © Kai Chiang; Page 4, 5, 10: © Yuri Arcurs; Page 6, 8, 12, 14, 18, 20: © Matthew Cole; Page 7: © Brad Calkins; Page 9: © Jérôme Berquez; Page 11: © Eileen Hart; Page 13: © benjaminmadison; Page 15: © Anneke Schram; Page 16: © Kathy Dewar; Page 17: © Tammy McAllister; Page 19: © deva;

Edited by Luana Mitten

Cover and Interior design by Teri Intzegian

Library of Congress Cataloging-in-Publication Data

Allen, Nancy Kelly
 Hopping on the Number Line / Nancy Kelly Allen.
     p. cm. -- (Little World Math)
 Includes bibliographical references and index.
 ISBN 978-1-61741-760-3 (hard cover) (alk. paper)
 ISBN 978-1-61741-962-1 (soft cover)
 Library of Congress Control Number: 2011924807

Rourke Publishing
Printed in the United States of America, North Mankato, Minnesota
060711
060711CL

www.rourkepublishing.com - rourke@rourkepublishing.com
Post Office Box 643328 Vero Beach, Florida 32964

Hop, hop, hop on the number line.
What is a number line?

A number line is
a line with numbers
placed in the right order.

0 1 2 3 4 5

Boing. Boing. Boing.

6 7 8 9 10 11

Hop onto number 3. Add 1 hop.

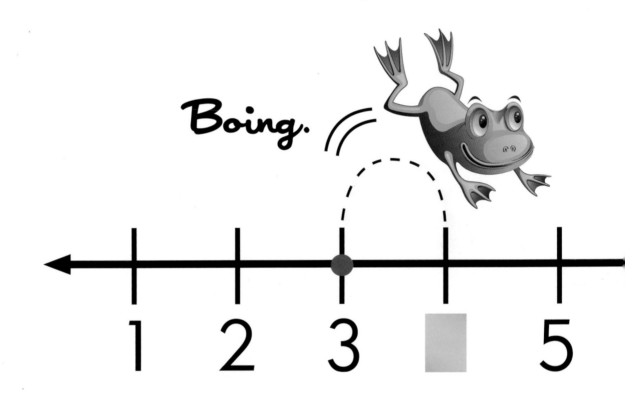

Boing.

1 2 3 ■ 5

$$3$$
$$+1$$
$$= ?$$

Plop down onto number

4

Start on number 12.
Add 3 hops.

Boing.
Boing.
Boing.

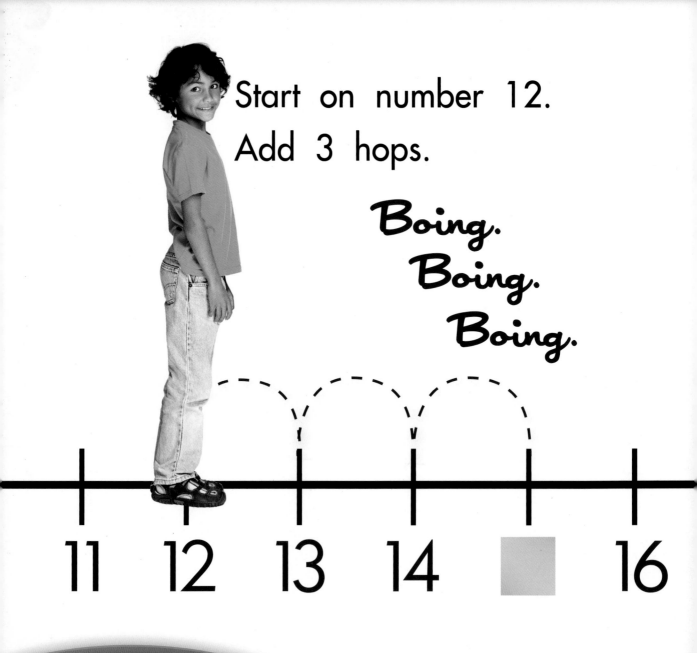

11 12 13 14 ▢ 16

$$12$$
$$+\ 3$$
$$=\ ?$$

Plop down onto number

Start on number 16. Subtract 2 hops.

$$\frac{16}{-2} = ?$$

Plop down onto number 14

Start on number 7. Add 3 hops.

Subtract 2 hops.

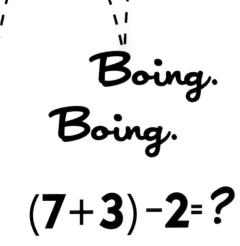

Boing.
Boing.

$(7+3)-2=?$

19

Plop down onto number

Can you find the right number on the number line?

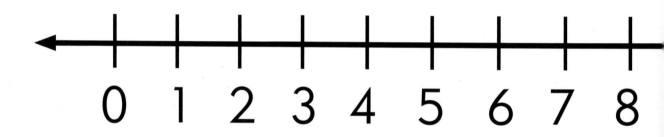

0 1 2 3 4 5 6 7 8

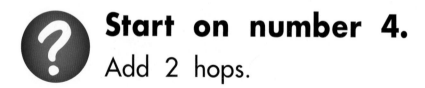

Start on number 4.
Add 2 hops.

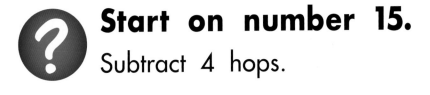

Start on number 15.
Subtract 4 hops.

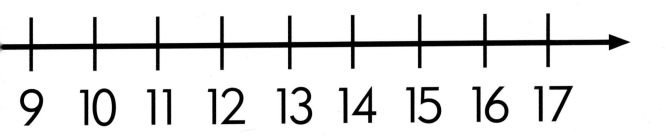

9 10 11 12 13 14 15 16 17

Start on number 11.
Add 4 hops. Subtract 4 hops.

Index

Websites

www.crickweb.co.uk/assets/resources/count-with-lecky7b.swf

www.funbrain.com/cgi-bin/nl.cgi?A1=s&A2=0

www.ictgames.com/frog.html [numberline]**

www.sheppardsoftware.com/mathgames/earlymath/
    BalloonPopMath_Order.htm

About the Author

Nancy Kelly Allen lives in Kentucky near a small creek. The creek has lots of flat rocks that are perfect for hopping across the water. Sometimes she hops across in three hops. And sometimes she adds one hop. Once, she hopped over a rock and plopped down in the water. Splash!